Wait! WHAT?

RUTH BADER GINSBURG
Couldn't
Drive?

DAN GUTMAN

illustrated by **ALLISON STEINFELD**

NORTON YOUNG READERS

An Imprint of W. W. Norton & Company
Celebrating a Century of Independent Publishing

To kids who like to learn cool stuff.

For information about permission to reproduce selections from this book, write to
Permissions, W. W. Norton & Company, Inc., 500 Fifth Avenue, New York, NY 10110

For information about special discounts for bulk purchases, please contact W. W. Norton
Special Sales at specialsales@wwnorton.com or 800-233-4830

Manufacturing by Lake Book Manufacturing
Book design by Patrick Collins
Production manager: Anna Oler

ISBN 978-1-324-03069-0 (cl)
978-1-324-03070-6 (pbk)

W. W. Norton & Company, Inc.,
500 Fifth Avenue, New York, N.Y. 10110
www.wwnorton.com

W. W. Norton & Company Ltd.,
15 Carlisle Street, London W1D 3BS

0 9 8 7 6 5 4 3 2 1

CONTENTS

That's True, But…

Hi everybody! My name is Paige, and this is my little brother Turner. Hey Turner, do you know what's really interesting?

Yeah, prunes. Think about it. They're sort of like grapes, but they're not grapes. And they're sort of like raisins, but they're not raisins either. What are they? They have a funny name and nobody likes them.

Turner you know perfectly well that nobody reading this cares about prunes.

But I do!

I'll tell you what's *really* interesting—famous people. Everybody likes to read about famous people. The problem is that biographies for kids always leave out the *good* stuff. The cool stuff.

Yeah, so we decided to learn about famous people and write about them. But we leave out all the boring junk and just include the good parts. Take Ruth Bader Ginsburg. Everybody knows that she was a famous Supreme Court justice. But did you know that she was a terrible driver?

Wait! WHAT? I didn't know that. How did you find that out?

I did my research, just like you! She failed her driving test *five* times before she was able to get her license. And one time, she hit Justice Sandra Day O'Connor's car in the Supreme Court parking garage!

I think the most amazing thing about that statement is that they have a Supreme Court parking garage. There are only nine members of the Supreme Court!

Yeah, can't they park on the street like normal people? I also found out that one time Ruth Bader Ginsburg crashed her car into a gate in Washington. After that, her husband drove her to the courthouse every day.

So *that's* the most interesting thing you found out about Ruth Bader Ginsburg?

Yes! I look up stuff that's interesting to *me*.

So I guess you didn't do a whole lot of serious research for this one, did you?

No, not really.

Well, I did *tons* of research on Ruth Bader Ginsburg. I dug up all kinds of cool facts that don't appear in other books for kids. Here's my favorite quote by her: "You can disagree without being disagreeable."

That's a good one. Look at the two of us. I *never* disagree with you.

You do too! You disagree with me all the time!

I do not!

You did it right there! You just proved my point!

Well, let's agree to disagree.

Okay.

See? We agreed to disagree. That proves *my* point.

You're impossible!

CHAPTER I

Stuff Your Teacher Wants You to Know About Ruth Bader Ginsburg...

March 15, 1933 Born in Flatbush, a
   neighborhood in Brooklyn, New York.

1946 Enters James Madison High School.

1950 Enters Cornell University.

1954 Graduates from Cornell,
   marries Martin Ginsburg.

1955 Daughter Jane is born.

1956 Ruth enters Harvard Law School.

1958 Transfers to Columbia Law School.

1959 Graduates from Columbia Law School.

1961–1963 Research associate and director at Columbia Law School.

1963–1972 Professor at Rutgers Law School.

1965 Son James is born.

1972 Co-founds the American Civil Liberties Union (ACLU) Women's Rights Project.

1972–1980 Professor at Columbia Law School.

1980 President Jimmy Carter appoints her as a judge for the United States Court of Appeals.

1986 Becomes a grandmother.

1993 President Bill Clinton appoints her to the Supreme Court.

2002 Inducted into the National Women's Hall of Fame.

2013 The Notorious R.B.G. blog appears.

2015 Is named one of *Time* magazine's most influential people.

2018 Becomes a great-grandmother.

2020 Dies on September 18 at age
eighty-seven.

Are you still awake? Fantastic! Okay, let's get to the *good* stuff, the stuff your *teacher* doesn't even know about Ruth Bader Ginsburg.

Wait! WHAT? I thought teachers know *everything*.

They know lots of stuff. But not *this* stuff!

"Young people should pursue something outside themselves, something they are passionate about: ending discrimination or keeping our planet safe, for example."

EQUAL RIGHTS

CHAPTER 2

Joan, Ruth, and Kiki

First things first. What should we call her? "Ruth Bader Ginsburg" is kind of a mouthful. I don't want to write that over and over again for a hundred pages.

What if we just call her Ruth?

I have news for you. Ruth wasn't her real name.

Wait! WHAT? It wasn't?

No. Her real name was Joan Bader.

Like Darth Vader?

Not Vader! *Bader!* Ruth was Joan's *middle* name.

Oh. So why did she go by her middle name?

When she started kindergarten, there were a few other girls in her class named Joan. Her mother suggested to the teacher that it would be less confusing if everybody called Joan by her middle name—Ruth.

Makes sense. So where did "Ginsburg" come from?

When she was older, she married a guy whose last name was Ginsburg. We'll get to him later.

How about we just call her "RBG" for short?

Works for me. But do you know what she was called when she was a baby?

Uh, Babe Ruth?

Very funny. Her nickname was "Kiki."

Kiki? Why?

Because she kicked a lot! Her older sister Marilyn said she was a "kicky baby."

I like "Kiki" better than "Ruth."

Me too. But sadly, when she was six years old, Marilyn caught a disease called meningitis, and she died. RBG was just fourteen months old at the time. So she grew up having no memory of her big sister.

That's sad. Hey, wait a minute. Aren't these books supposed to be funny?

Not always! Sometimes we have tragedy in life, Turner. There's going to be some funny stuff in this book, but there's going to be sadness too.

Okay, okay, chill.

44 BC Julius Caesar is assassinated.

1820 Maine is admitted as the twenty-third state.

1869 The Cincinnati Red Stockings become the first professional baseball team.

1892 The first escalator is patented by Jesse W. Reno in New York City.

1907 Finland becomes the first European country to give women the right to vote.

1913 Woodrow Wilson gives the first presidential press conference.

1930 The first seaplane glider takes off in Port Washington, New York.

1985 The first internet domain name is registered.

2019 Climate change strikes are held by kids all over the world, inspired by Swedish teenager Greta Thunberg.

2021 Deb Haaland, the first Native American to hold a United States cabinet position, is confirmed as Secretary of the Interior.

RBG grew up poor. Neither of her parents went to college. Her father, Nathan, was thirteen when he and his family came to Brooklyn, New York, from Russia. He had no money and he went to night school to learn how to speak English. He worked at his father's fur store. RBG's mother's name was Celia, and she came from Poland.

But she wasn't born in Poland.

Huh? How could she come from Poland if she wasn't born there?

Because Celia was inside her mother on the boat to America! She was born four months later.

Aha!

Here's another fun fact I found. RBG's father's brother married RBG's mother's sister.

Wait. I think my head's going to explode. Is that for real?

Yeah, I looked it up.

You look up weird stuff. Anyway, Celia got a job

as a bookkeeper, but she stopped working when she married Nathan.

How come?

In those days, most women didn't work. If a woman had a job, it meant her husband couldn't support her.

Man, the good old days were messed up.

Yeah. But even though the Baders were poor themselves, some years they had RBG's birthday party at an orphanage. They wanted less fortunate kids to have a good time and get ice cream.

Girls And Boys

RBG went to P.S. 238 in Brooklyn.

What does P.S. stand for? Pretty Silly?

No! Public School!

Oh. Duh!

She really liked playing dodgeball in gym class and recess. But she didn't like math or home economics.

Home economics? What's that? Did they teach kids how to buy houses?

No! Home economics was all about learning how to cook, sew, and stuff like that. In those days, all the girls would take home economics and all the boys would take shop.

Shop? They taught the boys how to go shopping?

No! Shop class was where boys would build stuff, like lamps, napkin holders, and things like that.

I'd rather build stuff than learn how to cook or sew.

I like building stuff *and* sewing. But when she was in eighth grade, the girls had to sew their own graduation dress. "Mine was a mess," RBG said. So her mother took the dress to a professional dressmaker to fix it.

"I liked shop better than cooking and sewing.... The boys used to make things out of wood, and I thought that was fun, to use the saw, and I didn't think it was fun to sew."

WWRRRRRR

Reading Can Be Dangerous

After RBG's sister died, their mother was extra-careful to keep RBG healthy. Whenever she got the sniffles, RBG had to stay home from school.

Gee, I wish our mom was like that. I'd stay home all the time.

You would not! One thing RBG and her mom liked to do most was read. One time RBG's mom was reading a book as she walked down the street in New York City, and she tripped and broke her nose.

See? That proves that reading can be hazardous to your health.

Very funny. Once a week, RBG and her mom would go on a "Friday afternoon adventure." Her mother's beauty parlor was in the same building as the local library. So while her mother was getting her hair done, RBG would sit in the library, reading her favorite books like *Little Women*, *Mary Poppins*, *The Secret Garden*, and the Nancy Drew mysteries. Later, she liked to read about her heroes, Anne Frank and Amelia Earhart.

Hey, we wrote about Amelia Earhart! She was cool.

She was. RBG also admired her mother, who always encouraged her to be strong and independent. One time RBG brought home a B on a math test and her mom was really disappointed. After that, RBG promised herself she would never bring home anything less than straight A's on her report card. And she never did.

"Reading is the key that opens doors to many good things in life."

Did you know that RBG and her mother were both left-handed?

So what?

Only one out of every ten people is a lefty.

But there have been plenty of famous left-handers.

FAMOUS LEFTIES!

Oprah Winfrey, Neil Armstrong,
Leonardo da Vinci, Michelangelo,
Paul McCartney, Napoleon Bonaparte,
Barack Obama, Lady Gaga, Bill Gates,
Jimi Hendrix, Charlie Chaplin,
Morgan Freeman, Lewis Carroll, Joan of Arc,
Mozart, Helen Keller, Babe Ruth,
Pierre and Marie Curie, Aristotle,
Harpo Marx, Julius Caesar, Judy Garland,
Kurt Cobain, David Bowie,
Mother Teresa.

There may have been a lot of famous lefties, but when RBG was a kid, many people thought there was something wrong with being left-handed, and lefties should be converted to right-handers.

That's messed up.

RBG's teacher forced her to write with her right hand. RBG cried, and she got a D on a penmanship test. After that, she decided she would never write another word with her right hand. She also decided not to let anybody force her to change the way she was.

World War II

RBG was eight years old in December 1941. She was on a Sunday drive with her parents, sitting in the backseat of the car. The radio was on.

I bet I know what happened next. Suddenly the program was interrupted with an announcement that Pearl Harbor in Hawaii had been attacked. The next day, America was at war.

Right. Everybody pitched in to help win World

War II, even kids. RBG helped plant a victory garden at school, and she helped knit blankets for the troops.

She also chewed lots of gum.

Wait! WHAT? How did chewing gum help the war effort?

CHEW CHEW

1¢ CHEW FOR THE TROOPS Bubble gum

Kids would peel the tinfoil off gum wrappers and make them into balls. These were used to build planes and tanks and stuff. It was called an "Aluminum for Defense" drive.

Why did they put aluminum in gum wrappers in the first place?

I don't know! But a few months after she turned twelve, America dropped the atomic bomb on Japan. A few weeks later, the war was over.

The next year, RBG was the editor of her school newspaper, *Highway Herald*. Do you know what she wrote about?

The glee club? Sports? Going to the circus?

No. She wrote about the atomic bomb.

That was my next guess.

This is what she wrote . . .

" . . . now we have a weapon that can destroy the world. We children of public school age can do much to aid in the promotion of peace. We must try to train ourselves and those about us to live together with one another as good neighbors . . . It is the only way to secure the world against future wars and maintain an everlasting peace. "

Wow. She sounds pretty smart for a twelve-year-old kid.

So I guess it's no surprise that RBG was ranked first in her eighth-grade class.

Do you think she was a nerd?

You tell me. She liked to ride her bike, roller-skate, jump rope, go horseback riding and waterskiing. She used to climb up on the top of her garage and jump from roof to roof.

Okay, maybe she wasn't such a nerd after all.

She also loved playing jacks and stoopball.

Jacks? You mean that thing they use to change the tire on a car?

No. Jacks is a game where you bounce a little ball while scooping up a bunch of little metal things in one hand.

Why would anybody want to do that?

Because it was fun!

What about stoopball? What's that?

You'd play it on the front stoop of your house. You'd throw a ball against the steps and try to make it so the fielders behind you couldn't catch the ball on a fly.

Jacks and stoopball sound like boring games. If I were growing up in those days, I'd be sitting around waiting for video games to be invented.

23

Well, in those days the streets of Brooklyn were *filled* with kids playing those boring games— Italian kids, Irish kids, black kids, white kids, Jewish kids, Polish kids—

Okay, I get it. All different kinds of kids.

Some of those kids didn't like RBG or her family.

Why not?

Because the Baders were Jewish.

What's wrong with being Jewish?

24

Nothing. Sometimes people just don't like other people who are different from them. Jews would be made fun of. Worse than that, lots of colleges, private clubs, and resorts didn't let Jewish people join, or they limited the number that would be admitted.

Just because they were Jewish?

Yes. One day, RBG was on a family drive in rural Pennsylvania when she saw a sign in front of an inn that said NO DOGS OR JEWS ALLOWED. She always remembered that.

I don't get it. Why would you dislike somebody just because they belong to a different religion?

Are you serious, Turner? It's almost a hundred years later, and many people *still* feel that way about people who have a different religion, nationality, or skin color.

I've never understood how anybody could dislike somebody they don't know.

Me neither.

26

CHAPTER 3

RBG Was a Go-Getter

RBG was popular in high school. She played cello in the school orchestra, and she was a twirler.

Twirler? What's that? Somebody who spins around in circles?

No! They twirl batons and throw them up in the air. One time, RBG chipped her front tooth on a baton while she was twirling.

Couldn't we try the debate team?

Ouch.

She was also a member of the Go-Getters Club.

I'm almost afraid to ask what that was.

It was a kind of student pep group. I guess they went and got stuff.

Here's an amazing fact: In RBG's high school yearbook, it was predicted that one of the seniors would become a Supreme Court justice.

Really? And it was RBG?

No! It was some guy named Joel Sheinbaum!

Obviously, he was never on the Supreme Court.

I think I'll take that, thank you very much.

Heh heh

Nah, he became a dentist.

That's funny. I hate to bring up more tragedy, but right after RBG started high school, her mother was diagnosed with cancer.

Yeah, I remember reading about that. And they didn't have chemotherapy or other modern treatments back then.

All through high school, RBG never told her classmates that her mother was sick. Then, two days before RBG's graduation, her mother died. Just four of the eight hundred seniors were asked to speak at graduation, and RBG was one of them.

But she didn't even go to her own graduation. She stayed home to be with her dad.

Campus Bathrooms

Back in 1950, hardly any young women went to college. But learning had been really important to RBG's mom, and after she died, RBG found out that her mom had saved eight thousand dollars to pay for her education.

Celia had put the money into five different bank accounts.

Why?

She had lived through the stock market crash and the bank failures of 1929. So she was afraid to put that much money in just one bank.

RBG ended up getting a full scholarship to Cornell University, in Ithaca, New York. And here's a fun fact: while she was at Cornell, one of RBG's professors was Vladimir Nabokov.

Vladimir *who*?

Nabokov. He wrote a really famous novel called *Lolita*. Taking a class with Nabokov made RBG a better writer. That would come in handy later, when she had to do a lot of writing as a member of the Supreme Court.

Do you want my autograph?

RBG was one of just a few girls at Cornell, and back then college was a different world than it is today. Girls were expected to wear skirts and flat shoes in classes. When they went to church or a nice luncheon, they had to wear white gloves and a hat. The Cornell library had separate entrances for males and females. And the girls had to be in their dormitory by ten o'clock every night or they would be punished.

Wait, tell me again why they called it the good old days?

Yeah, right? In those days, girls weren't supposed to look *too* smart. They would get teased if they spent a lot of time studying or reading. Many girls would hide how smart they were. The goal for a girl wasn't to get good grades or start a successful career. It was to find a husband who could support her.

"For most girls growing up in the 1940s, the most important degree was not your B.A., but your MRS."

That's unbelievable!

But it's true. In fact, many girls dropped out of college as soon as a boy proposed marriage to them.

Something tells me RBG wouldn't do that.

She would actually go study in the bathroom, because boys wouldn't bother her in there. She knew the location of every women's bathroom on the Cornell campus. But even so, she did meet a guy and fall in love.

Oh no, here comes the mushy stuff.

CHAPTER 4

The Mushy Stuff

It was the fall of 1950. RBG was seventeen, a freshman at Cornell. Marty Ginsburg was a sophomore. They were set up on a blind date to go to a formal dance. So romantic, right?

Not exactly. Later, Marty said, "The truth is, it was only a blind date on Ruth's side. I cheated. I asked a classmate to point her out in advance." He also said, "She's really cute. And, boy, she's really, really smart."

RBG and Marty were opposites. He was outgoing and funny. She was quiet and serious. He was tall. She was *tiny*—barely five feet, maybe a hundred pounds.

Sometimes opposites attract, like magnets.

Huh?

Magnets have two poles, north and south. If you take the south pole of one magnet and the north pole of another magnet, they—

Hey, wait a minute! We're not here to talk about magnets! You're getting off track. We were talking about RBG.

Okay, okay!

She had gone out on dates with other guys, but Marty was smarter than them, and he also liked her because *she* was smart. She said, "He was the only guy I ever dated who cared whether I had a brain."

At Cornell, RBG majored in government. She wanted to become a lawyer. Marty majored in chemistry. But mostly, he majored in golf.

Tell me more about the inequities in our legal system.

When he found out that his chemistry classes were at the same time as the Cornell golf team practice, he dropped chemistry and started taking law classes.

That way he could spend time with RBG and use her notes when he cut class.

He was pretty smart *too*.

Anyway, in June 1954 they got married in Marty's parents' living room. It was a few days after RBG graduated from Cornell. Eighteen people were at the wedding.

What difference does it make how many people were there?

In Judaism, the number eighteen symbolizes life.

Aha.

So at the wedding, RBG's new mother-in-law pulled her aside and said she was going to tell her the secret to a happy marriage.

What was it?

It's a secret!

Come on!

Okay, okay. She handed RBG a set of earplugs and said, "Dear, in every good marriage, it helps sometimes to be a little deaf."

What does that mean?

It means that when somebody says something mean or thoughtless to you, you should just tune it out. Getting angry doesn't make the situation better.

Hey, maybe you and I should try that. You're always saying mean things to me.

I'm going to pretend I didn't hear that.

"Don't be distracted by emotions like anger, envy, resentment. These just zap energy and waste time."

Hey, do you know what Marty's parents gave RBG as a wedding present?

A set of matching silverware? A lawn mower? A bag of cheese-flavored popcorn?

Golf clubs.

That was my next guess. So RBG graduated from Cornell with the highest honors. She and Marty were accepted into Harvard Law School. And guess what happened a year later?

They quit law school to become professional golfers?

No! They had a baby! A girl named Jane.

Oh yeah. And they were such clueless parents that they didn't even know how to give Jane a bath. It was Marty who suggested they put her in the kitchen sink.

Their marriage was an equal partnership. Marty did half the shopping, child care, and household chores. RBG took care of Jane while Marty was advancing in his career, and later he moved to Washington when she was advancing in her career.

But in the meantime, they both went to law school to become lawyers. RBG would go to classes and study until four o'clock in the afternoon. Then she'd play silly games and sing funny songs with the baby. After Jane fell asleep for the night, RBG would go back to studying.

It wasn't easy, but they made it work. Years later, when she was a respected judge and had to make lots of important decisions, RBG would tell people that the best decision she ever made was marrying Marty.

Cooking and Thinking

Let's talk about cooking.

Why? Because RBG was a woman? Because women are supposed to do all the cooking?

No. Because RBG was a terrible cook.

That's not very nice to say.

Maybe, but it's true. RBG's idea of cooking a meal was to make Jell-O and cottage cheese.

Ugh. I think I'm going to throw up.

She learned how to cook seven dishes. After she made the seventh meal, she would go back to number one and cook that again. Early in their marriage, RBG made a tuna casserole. Marty took one look at it and asked, "What is it?" So do you know what he did?

He threw it in the garbage?

No. He learned how to cook! And it turned out he was *really* good at it. Besides cooking fantastic meals, he was famous for his chocolate chip oatmeal cookies. And he would bake a cake whenever RBG won a big case or one of her friends had a birthday.

Maybe his interest in chemistry came in handy for cooking.

Maybe. When Jane grew up, she would say her parents divided the household chores equally— her father did the cooking and her mother did the thinking.

CHAPTER 5

The Good Old Days

Okay, so it was 1955, and RBG was in law school. But it wasn't going to be easy. She had four strikes against her. She was taking care of a baby. She was Jewish. She was tiny, and didn't *look* like a lawyer. And of course—

She was a woman. The Constitution starts with the words "We the people." But it left out a *lot* of people—Native Americans, enslaved people, and women, who make up half the population. It wasn't fair!

Wait. Didn't we learn in school that the Fourteenth Amendment says everyone should be treated equally? That was passed way back in 1868.

Yeah, but women weren't treated as full legal citizens. We weren't even allowed to *vote* until 1920, just thirteen years before RBG was born. When RBG started law school, she was one of just nine women in a class of 552 students. There were no women professors, and they didn't even have a ladies' bathroom in the building where classes were held. The female students had to walk a block to use the bathroom.

That's not fair.

One of RBG's professors actually asked her, "Why are you at Harvard Law School, taking a place that could have gone to a man?"

Wow. It's hard to believe the world was like that, and not very long ago.

You want to hear some statistics?

No. I hate statistics.

Too bad. From 1947 to 1967, less than five percent of all law students were women. In the early 1960s, only three percent of American lawyers were women. And Yale, which started way back in 1701, didn't even admit *any* female students until 1969.

Okay, okay! No more stats!

One more thing. In 1911, the students at the University of Pennsylvania Law School decided it would be a great idea to have all the freshmen grow mustaches. Just before they were about to vote on it, somebody remembered that there was a woman in the class. So they called off the vote.

Okay, I get it. Things were tough for women in the good old days.

RBG was a short, skinny, quiet little lady, but she was *tough*. She was a tiger. Some of the students called her "Ruthless Ruthie." She raised her daughter and finished law school as one of the top students in her class. When she was handed her diploma, four-year-old Jane shouted, "That's my mommy!"

I see the happy ending to this chapter coming. Don't tell me. Let me guess. RBG graduates from law school, becomes a high-powered lawyer, and she gets picked to become a Supreme Court Justice. Right?

Nice try, but no. After she finished law school, not one law firm offered her a job.

What?!

So you know what she did?

She became a professional golfer?

No. She wrote a book about the legal system in Sweden.

Oh. I didn't see *that* coming.

Yeah, she spent a year learning Swedish and studying Swedish law. Her first book was *Civil Procedure in Sweden*. But after that, she decided that she wanted to do something to fight for women's equality. So you know what she did?

She led protest marches? She posted angry messages on social media?

No. Protest marches weren't her thing. And there *was* no social media back then.

Oh right. It was before the internet. They didn't even have personal computers back then. So what did she do?

I'll tell you in the next chapter.

What a tease!

THINGS WOMEN COULDN'T DO
in the 1930s and 1940s

MISSING

THE REST OF MY PAYCHECK

Nice try!

+ Be a lawyer or judge in most states.

+ Get paid the same amount as men doing the same work.

+ Apply for jobs labeled "men only."

+ Attend most Ivy League colleges.

+ Serve on a jury in most states.

+ Play school sports on an equal basis with guys.

+ Open a bank account without her husband or a male relative's permission.

+ Get a credit card without her husband or a male relative's permission.

+ Own property in some states without having a husband in control as "head and master."

+ Get pregnant without the threat of losing her job.

+ Wear pants on the Senate floor.

+ Go to military school.

+ Serve in combat in the military.

CHAPTER 6

Genius Strategy

🧑 Hey, Paige, do you like prunes?

👩 No! What is it with you and prunes? What do prunes have to do with anything?

🧑 I was just wondering if you like prunes.

👩 What difference does it make? Why would you waste time in the middle of the book to ask me if I like prunes?

Sheesh, sis, lighten up!

Can we move on? After she got her law degree in 1959, RBG and Marty moved to Oklahoma for a couple of years. Marty had joined the Army and RBG got a job at the Social Security Administration.

After that, Marty started his career as a lawyer. RBG became a law professor at Rutgers in 1963, and later at Columbia University. Then she became a lawyer with the American Civil Liberties Union. In 1965, they had another baby, a son named James.

I can't imagine what it must have been like to take care of two young kids while trying to start a career.

Ask Mom!

Wait. Wasn't 1965 when the hippies and all that sixties stuff started happening?

Yeah, change was in the air. The civil rights movement was in full swing. African Americans, Native Americans, gay people, and other groups were demanding equal rights. RBG and a lot

of others decided to fight for women's rights. But instead of marching and protesting, RBG thought the *law* could be used to change things.

What did she do?

Well, it would have been great to just convince the courts to rule that discrimination against women was illegal. Boom, done! But that would have been really hard to do, maybe impossible. RBG had a different strategy—to *gradually* change unfair laws until there would be justice for all people.

> **"Real change, enduring change, happens one step at a time."**

I don't get it.

She thought the Constitution might be the answer to women's equality. You mentioned the Fourteenth Amendment earlier . . .

The Fourteenth Amendment...

All persons born or naturalized in the United States, and subject to the jurisdiction thereof, are citizens of the United States and of the State wherein they reside. No State shall make or enforce any law which shall abridge the privileges or immunities of citizens of the United States . . .

Huh? Slow down. You lost me at "naturalized."

Basically, the Fourteenth Amendment says that anyone born in the United States is a citizen, and all citizens are equal.

So, if women born in the United States are citizens, and all citizens should be treated equally . . . then women should be treated equally to men.

Right! And get *this*. The way she changed the laws was to take on lawsuits representing *men*.

Huh, why?

If she could prove that a man was discriminated against simply because he was a man, the judges might rule that discrimination was illegal and men and women should be treated equally.

I still don't get it.

Let me give you an example of one case RBG took on. There was this New Jersey guy named Stephen Wiesenfeld. His wife Paula died during childbirth. So Stephen decided to stop working to take care of their newborn son.

What's wrong with that?

Nothing. Before she died, Paula, who was a math teacher, had paid money into Social Security with every one of her paychecks. When Stephen applied to Social Security to get survivor benefits, he was rejected.

Why?

Because he was a man. According to the law, a woman could collect from Social Security if her husband died, but a man couldn't collect if his wife died.

That's not fair.

No, it's not. And RBG won the case unanimously. She convinced the entire Supreme Court that discrimination hurt *everybody*, women *and* men.

Okay, now I get it. That is genius!

Little by little, one case at a time, RBG helped get rid of laws that were based on the idea that only men earned money and only women took care of their home and children.

Sounds like a no-brainer to me. Sometimes men take care of their kids, and sometimes women get jobs to support their families.

Right! RBG brought six women's rights cases to the Supreme Court, and she won five of them.

So winning those cases helped get rid of laws that discriminated against women.

Exactly! And when the laws changed, people's attitudes changed.

Paddle Boarding?

The other thing that made RBG so successful was that she worked her butt off. Can we use the word *butt* in a book for kids?

I don't know. If it ends up in the book, we'll know we were allowed to use it.

RBG worked so hard that Marty would have to call her up at work and remind her to come home for dinner. Then, after the kids were asleep, she would work until four o'clock in the morning. Her assistants got used to receiving messages from her in the middle of the night.

She was also famous for not needing much sleep. Sometimes she got just one or two hours a night. She drank a lot of coffee to stay awake.

Did you Google that picture of RBG when she fell asleep during the president's State of the Union speech?

That was hilarious. But she was also famous for being able to concentrate really hard on whatever she was doing. Her college roommate said, "You could drop a bomb over her head and she wouldn't know it."

One time, a bunch of people gathered in RBG's office to give her a birthday cake. She was so focused on the work she was doing that she didn't notice the room was filled with people until they started singing "Happy Birthday."

She worked really hard, but she still found time to dance, play piano, go to the movies, read, and play golf with Marty. In fact, she was so driven that she would get her reading done while she was sitting in the golf cart between strokes.

She also liked water-skiing, horseback riding, and white water rafting.

And don't forget paddle boarding.

Paddle boarding? What's that?

You stand on a board and paddle it.

You can't sit down?

I guess you *could* sit down if you wanted to.

That sounds like fun. Tell me more about paddle boarding.

Nice try, Turner! This book isn't about water sports! RBG was one of the most famous Supreme Court justices in history. So we should get to that part of her story.

Hey, *you're* the one who brought up paddle boarding! We should do a paddle boarding book someday. That would be cool.

"If you want your dreams to come true, you must be willing to put in the hard work it takes to make that possible."

CHAPTER 7

The Supreme Court

With each lawsuit she won, RBG was getting more respected and well known in the legal world. Her daughter Jane was in high school by the early 1970s, and in her yearbook she wrote that her ambition was to see her mom appointed to the Supreme Court.

I have a confession to make.

What?

I don't even know exactly what the Supreme Court *is*.

That's nothing to be ashamed of, Turner. It's the highest court in the land. That means it has the final say, and the decisions it makes can change history. Maybe this will help . . .

Stuff you don't know about
THE SUPREME COURT

+ There are nine judges, and they're called "justices."

+ They don't make laws. They interpret the laws made by Congress. So the justices decide which laws are fair and which ones aren't.

+ They use the Constitution as their guide.

+ They're asked to rule on thousands of cases each year, but they only take about seventy-five of them. They look for important cases about federal law where judges in lower courts disagree about what the law means.

+ The Supreme Court can change decisions made by lower courts, or decide a law is unconstitutional.

+ The justices are appointed for life. The only end to their career is when they retire, get impeached, or die.

+ No cameras are allowed inside the Supreme Court.

+ The newest member of the Court has to answer the phone, pour coffee, take messages, and open the door.

This feels like an injustice.

+ June is the Court's busiest time. That's when the justices issue their rulings before they recess for the summer.

They have recess all summer? Cool! Do they get to play on the Supreme Court monkey bars?

Funny.

Was RBG the first woman on the Supreme Court?

She was the *second*. For two centuries, there were only male justices. Then, in 1981, President Ronald Reagan appointed Sandra Day O'Connor, the first woman. And that's the way it was until 1993, when Justice Byron "Whizzer" White retired.

His name was Whizzer? Did he like to pee on stuff?

No, dope! When he was younger, he was a football player! He was nicknamed "Whizzer" because he could run really fast.

Get out!

It's true! He even played in the NFL and led the league in rushing for two seasons. Look it up!

Okay, okay! So when somebody retires or dies, the president picks a new justice to fill the spot.

Right. Bill Clinton was president when Byron White retired. There were a bunch of good candidates, and RBG wasn't considered to be high on the list. She was a sixty-year-old grandmother, which is kind of old to get started on the Supreme Court. But after thinking it over for a long time, President Clinton decided she was the best person for the job.

How come?

Well, RBG was really accomplished, plus Clinton said, "I liked the fact that she had a sense of humor."

I thought you said she was really serious all the time.

Well, Clinton thought RBG was funny. He decided he would call her with the good news after watching a basketball game on TV. But the game went into triple overtime. It was one of the longest games in NBA history. Finally it ended just before midnight, and the president made the call.

Did I wake you up?
—President Bill Clinton

But the president doesn't just decide all by himself, right?

Right, you have to be confirmed by the Senate. At her confirmation hearings, RBG held up a book her grandson Paul made. It was called "My Grandma Is Very Special."

I bet RBG charmed everybody.

The Senate voted 96–3 to confirm her, and on June 14, 1993, RBG became the 107th justice of the Supreme Court. First she thanked her mother, and then she thanked her daughter and son, because they "appreciate that Daddy cooks ever so much better than Mommy, and so phased me out of the kitchen at a relatively early age."

Here's a fun fact: While RBG was giving her acceptance speech, a young lawyer was in the crowd. Her name was Elena Kagan. Seventeen years later, *she* became a Supreme Court justice.

"People ask me sometimes . . . When will there be enough women on the court? And my answer is When there are nine."

So now there were *two* women on the Supreme Court, RBG and Sandra Day O'Connor.

Here's another fun fact: Sandra Day O'Connor is in the National Cowgirl Hall of Fame.

What? Where do you dig up this stuff?

I research the *important* stuff, okay? Here's something else I found out. In the twelve years Sandra Day O'Connor was the only woman on the Supreme Court, they never gave her a bathroom.

What, more bathroom facts?

Hey, I don't make this stuff up. It wasn't until RBG joined the Court that a women's bathroom was installed in the room where the justices put on their robes. Before that, when nature called, O'Connor had to run back to her office.

Also, lawyers appearing before the Court would often get O'Connor and RBG mixed up and call them by the other one's name.

As if all women look alike!

As a joke, the National Association of Women Judges printed up a T-shirt for each of them. RBG's shirt said I'M RUTH, NOT SANDRA and Justice O'Connor's shirt said I'M SANDRA, NOT RUTH.

O'Connor retired in 2006, and then RBG was the only woman on the Court. I bet she was lonely.

Oh, but she had a friend.

Nino!

RBG and Justice Antonin Scalia served on the Supreme Court together for twenty-three years. The two of them had almost completely opposite opinions on legal matters, but they liked debating, they respected each other, and they became good friends.

When Scalia was asked to name the one person he would want to be stranded with on a desert island, he replied, "Ruth Bader Ginsburg." And she said, "I love him, but sometimes I'd like to strangle him."

RBG's husband Marty hated shopping, but Justice Scalia would go shopping with her. Every year on her birthday, Scalia sent RBG roses, and their families would spend New Year's Eve and Thanksgiving together.

Scalia liked to hunt, and he would bring whatever animal he shot on his most recent hunting trip. Guests would say, "Scalia kills it. Marty cooks it."

The Scalias and Ginsburgs even went on vacations together. One time, they went parasailing, and Scalia joked that RBG was so light that she might never come back to earth.

On the other hand, Justice Scalia was a bit on the chubby side. In 1994 they took a trip to India, and photos appeared of them riding an elephant together. People asked RBG why *she* had to sit on the *back* of the elephant, and she said, "It had to do with the distribution of weight."

Oh snap. What a burn!

They were just joking. He called her his "best buddy." RBG and Scalia had one big common interest . . .

Opera!

Ugh, I hate opera.

This isn't about you, Turner. RBG loved music. "It's one of the things that makes life beautiful," she said. The only problem was, she was terrible at it.

That's not very nice to say.

But it's true. When she was a kid, RBG played piano and cello, but not very well. And when it came to singing, her music teacher told her to just mouth the words but not sing them.

Ouch! Major burn.

She and Justice Scalia both loved opera, and they would go the Washington National Opera together. A few times, they were invited to be part of a performance, and they got up onstage wearing powdered wigs and full costumes. Sometimes they had speaking parts. They even had an opera named after them.

Wait! WHAT?

In 2015, a law school student named Derrick Wang wrote an opera about two people who are totally different and they're locked in a room together. The only way out is for them to agree to a common approach on the Constitution. The opera was called *Scalia/Ginsburg* and it was based on their legal writings. The two characters sang a song titled "We Are Different, We Are One" about how much they love the Constitution.

On her seventy-fifth birthday, the opera superstar Placido Domingo sang "Happy Birthday" to RBG. It was one of the best days of her life. She said, "Being so close to that great voice was like having electric shock run through me."

CHAPTER 8

RBG, Rock Star

In 2013, RBG was eighty years old. Usually older women become sort of invisible in our society. But something amazing happened. When she was eighty, RBG became one of the most famous people in the world.

How did that happen?

A law student at New York University started a blog in honor of RBG. She called it "Notorious R.B.G." after a legendary rapper named Biggie Smalls.

Oh yeah, I heard of that guy. He called himself the Notorious B.I.G.

Right. Actually, RBG and BIG had something in common. They were both born and raised in Brooklyn.

And Biggie's first record came out in 1993, the same year RBG joined the Supreme Court.

Anyway, the blog went viral. It was made into a book too. Soon, RBG memes started appearing all over the place. RBG was giving a lecture at the University of California, and students showed up wearing T-shirts that said NOTORIOUS R.B.G., RUTH IS TRUTH, THE RUTH WILL SET YOU FREE, and RUTH BADER GINSBURG IS MY HOMEGIRL.

Things got crazy. There was an RBG comic book. A beer was named in her honor. At a school in Dallas, Texas, a class named their fish "Ruth Beta Ginsburg"!

After the press reported that RBG would read her mail with a little flashlight during previews of movies, people all over the country started sending her little flashlights!

Fifteen thousand people gave money to a Kickstarter campaign to make an RBG action figure!

OTHER RBG PRODUCTS
You Can Buy

coffee mugs

birthday cards

coloring books

nail decals

Valentine's Day cards

Halloween costumes

Christmas tree ornaments

socks • dolls

calendars • bottle openers

bobblehead dolls

pillows • earrings

bookmarks

bracelets • candles

tote bags

stickers

jigsaw puzzles

RBG IN MOVIES...

+ There was a Lego figurine of RBG in *The Lego Movie 2*.

+ In *Deadpool 2*, Deadpool considers RBG for his X-Force team of superheroes.

+ A movie about her titled *RBG* was nominated for Best Documentary Feature at the Oscars.

RBG ON TV...

+ On the Cartoon Network, they had an action figure named Wrath Hover Ginsbot who was "appointed for life to kick your butt."

+ In *The Good Place*, RBG was mentioned as the girlfriend of Drake, the Canadian rapper.

+ On *Saturday Night Live*, Kate McKinnon dressed up as RBG and danced around insulting people and shouting, "You just got Gins-burned!"

No other Supreme Court justice had ever caused a sensation like that. Suddenly this cute little old lady who looked like everybody's grandma was a huge celebrity and folk hero.

She was like a rock star! And speaking of rock stars, did you know that RBG had the same birthday—March 15—as Mike Love of the Beach Boys, Dee Snider of Twisted Sister, and Sly Stone of Sly and the Family Stone?

So what?

It's interesting! Also, President Andrew Jackson had the same birthday as RBG.

Everybody was going RBG-crazy! People were getting tattoos of her face.

Speaking of tattoos, did you read about that tattoo artist named Ari Richter?

No.

He had a habit of biting his cheek when he was nervous.

So? What does that have to do with RBG?

Well, he collected the skin that he bit off, and froze it.

Okay, that's kind of gross. But I don't see what that has to do with RBG.

Then he'd lay the frozen skin out on a piece of glass and dry it.

And?

Then he'd use ink to make a picture . . . of RBG!

Wait! WHAT?

That's not all. RBG officiated at the tattoo artist's wedding. And do you know who he married?

Who?

Irin Carmon, one of the authors of the book *Notorious RBG*!

What's a Jabot?

Here's a fun fact. When RBG joined the Supreme Court, *People* magazine put her on their list of "America's Worst Dressed." Twenty years later, she was one of *Glamour* magazine's "Women of the Year."

Wait a minute. Are you going to talk about RBG's clothing now? If she were a man, we wouldn't be talking about what *he* wore.

Hey, if RBG were a man, we probably wouldn't be talking about him at *all*.

Fair enough. Actually, RBG made some interesting fashion choices. She went to a lot of receptions and other places where she had to shake lots of hands, so she started wearing black or white lace gloves. And sometimes she wore a turban.

Why?

Who knows? Anyway, she didn't have her ears pierced, but she wore dangling clip-on earrings. And she combed her dark blond hair back and wore a scrunchie.

I give up. What's a scrunchie?

You really don't know what a scrunchie is? Everybody knows what a scrunchie is.

I don't, okay?

It's this little cloth thing with elastic that you use to hold hair in a ponytail.

I always wondered what that thing was called.

RBG had a collection of them. When she was sworn in as a Supreme Court justice she wore a blue scrunchie. But RBG was *most* famous for her collection of jabots.

Oh no. Is that something *else* I'm supposed to know about? What's a jabot, some kind of a robot?

No, it's a decorative collar you hang around your neck. You see, all the Supreme Court justices wear the same boring black robe. The robes were designed for men,  so their shirt and tie show through at the top. RBG decided to accessorize her robe with a fancy French lace jabot, and she had a whole collection of them. People would send them to her.

Sounds like a good idea.

Here's the thing. The justices don't always agree on rulings. Sometimes they're in the majority, and sometimes they're in the minority.

So?

So RBG would wear one jabot when she issued a majority ruling, and a different jabot when she issued a minority ruling, which is called a "dissent."

For real?

It's true. When she was in the majority, she would wear a lace jabot with gold trim and charms on it. When she gave a dissenting opinion, she wore a jabot with mirrored glass beads and black velvet.

I guess people knew what her opinion was going to be depending on which jabot she was wearing.

Exactly! And after RBG started wearing jabots, Chief Justice William Rehnquist put four gold stripes on the arm of his robe in honor of a character in his favorite opera.

Those Supreme Court justices were so fashionable!

Ya gotta keep up with the Ginsburgs. And here's a fun fact: In 2016, scientists at the Cleveland Museum of Natural History had the chance to name a species of praying mantis from Madagascar. Do you know what they named it?

Jabot?

No, they named it *Ilomantis ginsburgae*, because its neck plate looked like RBG's jabot.

Okay, that's just weird.

The RBG Workout

As she got older, RBG started slowing down and having health problems. She had to give up waterskiing, parasailing, and horseback riding. But she realized she needed to stay in shape. She tried taking Jazzercise classes, but she didn't like them because the music was so loud. So she decided to hire a personal trainer.

His name was Bryant Johnson. He was an Army Reserve sergeant and a paratrooper. Big strong guy. Over two hundred pounds. He could do eighty-four push-ups in two minutes. RBG started working out with Bryant twice a week at the Supreme Court gym.

Wait. So they have a parking garage *and* a gym for just nine justices?

I guess so. Bryant Johnson had RBG doing planks, push-ups, bench presses, one-legged squats, and they would toss a twelve-pound medicine ball back and forth. She was eighty, and she could do more than twenty push-ups! Bryant Johnson said she was T.A.N—tough as nails.

 Photos appeared of RBG working out in her SUPER DIVA sweatshirt. She was so inspiring that Bryant Johnson's mother started exercising too, and she lost fifty pounds.

Working out with RBG made Bryant Johnson famous. In 2017, he wrote a book called *The RBG Workout: How She Stays Strong . . . and You Can Too!*

"If I go somewhere and talk about myself, I don't learn anything. If I listen to other people, more likely than not, I will find out something I didn't know."

CHAPTER 9

More Tragedy

I can see we're coming to the end of the book. There aren't many pages left.

We should probably talk about how RBG changed America. Remember back in Chapter Five when I said in the early sixties only three percent of all lawyers were women? Well, now it's about thirty percent. And about half of all law students in America are women now. I also said that Yale didn't admit any female students until 1969. In 2020, women outnumbered men at Yale!

Enough stats. I get it. Today, *lots* of women are judges, presidents of top universities, and members of Congress. Kamala Harris was our first female vice president.

Of course, you can't give RBG credit for all those things. *Lots* of people fought really hard to get equal rights for women.

I guess it's time for us to start wrapping this thing up. I always feel a little sad when we get to the ending of these books.

Because the project is almost over?

No, because the person we're writing about is gonna die.

Oh yeah. More tragedy. RBG was just a year old when her sister died. She was thirteen when her mother got cancer and she died when RBG was finishing high school.

Her husband Marty beat cancer when he was in his twenties, and then he got it again in his seventies. He died in 2010. They had been married for fifty-six years.

And the day after Marty died, RBG was at the Supreme Court like any other day to announce one of the Court's decisions. She was so strong. She was diagnosed with cancer in 1999 and she didn't miss a day of work. She got it again in 2009, and beat it again.

Then, at the end of 2018, RBG had a fall and broke three ribs. The doctors took X-rays, and they found some growths on her lungs. She died of pancreatic cancer on September 18, 2020. She was eighty-seven.

When RBG died, the country went into mourning. She was the first woman—and the first Jewish person—to lie in state at the United States Capitol. She and Marty are buried next to one another in Arlington National Cemetery.

CHAPTER 10

Oh Yeah? (Stuff About RBG That Didn't Fit Anywhere Else)

Okay, what do you have left in your notes, Turner?

Let me see. Oh, I know something you don't know, Paige. One time RBG appeared on Stephen Colbert's TV show. He asked her to make a judgment about a very important question—"Is a hot dog a sandwich?" RBG decided that yes, a hot dog *is* a sandwich.

Speaking of Stephens, remember that guy Stephen Wiesenfeld whose wife died during childbirth and RBG took on his case to get him Social Security benefits? Well, when their baby Jason grew up, RBG performed his wedding ceremony. And when Stephen remarried, RBG performed *his* wedding ceremony too!

Supreme Court justices often perform wedding ceremonies for friends and relatives. In 2013 RBG became the first justice to perform a same-sex marriage.

Oh yeah? Try this. For her seventy-fifth birthday, RBG was asked to name one person she'd like to record a special birthday message for her. She picked Joe Torre, the manager of the New York Yankees, who also came from Brooklyn. But RBG wasn't a big sports fan. One time, there was a parade down Constitution Avenue in Washington, D.C. RBG asked her secretary why there was so much noise outside. The secretary told her Washington had won the Super Bowl. And do you know what RBG said?

"What's the Super Bowl?"

Right!

Do you know what RBG carried in her purse at all times?

A wallet?

Well, maybe. But she also carried a copy of the Constitution. And did you know RBG's favorite artist was Henri Matisse?

Everybody knows that. Did you know that besides being a terrible driver, she was also a lousy typist?

Oh yeah? I bet you don't know this. When she was thirteen, some friends dared RBG to take a puff of a cigarette without coughing. She did it, and became addicted to smoking for forty years.

I never saw a picture of her with a cigarette.

I guess she was careful not to smoke in public.

Did you ever hear of the Watergate scandal? RBG lived in the Watergate Hotel part of the time she spent in Washington.

Marty Ginsburg became one of the top tax lawyers in the country, but it was RBG who kept track of the family's financial records.

Speaking of Marty, he liked to joke around a lot, and he convinced his kids Jane and James that the bronze statue at the top of the Capitol dome was a statue of *him*. Actually, the *Statue of Freedom* is a *woman*, with a helmet and a sword in her hand.

Marty was hilarious, but RBG had a reputation for being very serious. Jane and James would try to make her laugh, and every time they did, Jane would make a mark in a book called *Mommy Laughed*. RBG's good friend Justice Scalia said, "A lot of people have this notion that she is a sourpuss, and she is not. She's a pussycat."

After Marty died, the wives of some of the other Supreme Court justices published a collection of his best recipes. It was titled *Chef Supreme*.

Jane Ginsburg grew up to become a lawyer like her parents. RBG and Jane were the first mother and daughter to both attend Harvard Law School.

Oh yeah? RBG's grandson Paul Spera is an actor who has appeared in lots of plays and movies.

I bet you didn't find this. In 2011, RBG was about to take off on a flight from Washington to San Francisco when the pilot noticed smoke coming out of one of the plane's engines. So seventy-eight-year-old RBG and all the other passengers had to slide down an inflatable chute to safety.

RBG was known to be a very slow eater. Friends would say that world wars could be finished before she could finish her appetizer.

Yum!

She was also known to be a very slow *talker*. When she was

speaking, there would often be long pauses in the middle of her sentences. She said, "I try to think before I speak."

This has nothing to do with RBG, but it's a good one. The longest-serving Supreme Court justice was William O. Douglas. He was on the Court for more than thirty-six years. The justice who spent the shortest time on the bench was Thomas Johnson. He died after just 163 days.

At the start of each day, the Supreme Court justices all shake hands with each other. At ten a.m., a buzzer sounds in the Court and everybody stands up. The marshall of the Supreme Court shouts, "Oyez, oyez, oyez."

What does *that* mean?

It's sort of like, "Hear ye, hear ye."

And what does *that* mean?

It means everybody is supposed to shut up.

Why don't they just say, "Everybody shut up"?

That would be rude! But did you know there's a basketball court at the Supreme Court?

So I guess it's the Supreme Court court. Wait, they have a parking garage, a gym, *and* a basketball court? Those justices have it good.

Yeah. President Obama loved playing basketball. When he was invited to play on the Supreme Court court, he said, "I don't know. I hear that Justice Ginsburg has been working on her jump shot."

Get this. In the Supreme Court, each justice has a green spittoon next to his or her seat.

What's a spittoon?

It's a bowl you spit into.

Wait! WHAT? Gross! You've got to be joking.

No, it's for real. A hundred years ago, lots of men chewed tobacco, and they would spit the juice into a spittoon. They were everywhere—in bars, stores, hotels, banks, and even in the Supreme Court.

You mean to say they don't allow TV cameras in the Supreme Court, but you're free to spit in there?

Well, these days the Supreme Court spittoons are used as wastebaskets.

Why don't they just get regular wastebaskets?

It's a tradition! Hey, speaking of gross stuff, before she was a member of the Supreme Court, RBG appeared before the court as a lawyer. On the day of one of her first cases, she skipped lunch because she was so nervous she thought she might throw up.

Ooh, I think this is the last page!

Wait! There's one more thing we need to talk about. Do you know what was RBG's favorite snack?

Pretzels?

No.

Popcorn?

No.

Cheez Doodles?

No.

Don't tell me. I don't want to know. Okay, okay, what was it?

Prunes!

You're impossible!

TO FIND OUT MORE...

Did we get you interested in the life of Ruth Bader Ginsburg? Yay! You may want to check out a few of the more serious children's books about her, like *No Truth without Ruth* by Kathleen Krull, and *I Dissent: Ruth Bader Ginsburg Makes Her Mark* by Debbie Levy and Elizabeth Baddeley. Ask your librarian if you can't find them.

There are also videos about RBG on YouTube.

ACKNOWLEDGMENTS

Thanks to Simon Boughton, Kristin Allard, Liza Voges, Nina Wallace, and Allison Steinfeld. The facts in this book came from various books, websites, and other sources. Especially helpful was *My Own Words: Ruth Bader Ginsburg* with Mary Hartnett and Wendy W. Williams, *Ruth Bader Ginsburg: A Life* by Jane Sherron De Hart, *Conversations with RBG: Ruth Bader Ginsburg on Life, Love, Liberty, and Law* by Jeffrey Rosen, and *Notorious R.B.G* by Irin Carmon and Shana Knizhnik.

ABOUT THE AUTHOR

Dan Gutman has written many books for young readers, such as the My Weird School series, *Houdini and Me*, The Genius Files, Flashback Four, *The Kid Who Ran for President*, *The Homework Machine*, *The Million Dollar Shot*, and his baseball card adventure series. Dan and his wife, Nina, live in New York City. You can find out more about Dan and his books by visiting his website (www.dangutman.com) or following him on Facebook, Twitter, and Instagram.

TITLES IN THE

Wait! WHAT?

SERIES